LITTLE BOATS,
UNSALVAGED

LITTLE BOATS, UNSALVAGED

POEMS, 1992–2004

DAVE SMITH

LOUISIANA STATE UNIVERSITY PRESS

BATON ROUGE

DESIGNER: Andrew Shurtz   TYPEFACE: Bembo
PRINTER AND BINDER: Edwards Brothers, Inc.

The author wishes to thank the editors of these publications for first printing poems named here, often in different versions: *Aethlon: A Journal of Sport Literature:* "Vacant Lot" (Spring 2004); *American Poetry Review:* "In the Pre-Alps," "Brown Lizards," "One Religious Life," "Dividing Jerusalem" (all March–April 2003); *Five Points:* "Malamud's Books Half-Priced" (Winter 1997), "Allegheny Happiness" (Winter 1999), "Aunt Pink and Uncle Brownie's Day" and "Flamingo Film" (both forthcoming); *Georgia Review:* "Plowman" (Summer 2003), "Warren's Flowers" (Spring 2004), "The Clam-Rake Room," "Gene Vincent's Blue Cap," "The Altar," "Seeking Words," "The Quail Men of Churchland," "Bad Waters," "Milan Cathedral Eclipse," "Last Supper" (all Winter 2004); *Harvard Magazine:* "Little Boats, Unsalvaged" (September–October 2004; presented as the 223rd Harvard University Phi Beta Kappa Poem on June 8, 2004); *Meridian:* "Play," "Oyster Beds" (both Spring–Summer 2004); *New Republic:* "Beagles, Hunters" (January 26, 2004); *Nightsun:* "Casteen's Pure Oil Station" (January 2005); *North American Review:* "Can of Beans" (July–August 1994); *Poems for a Small Planet,* edited by Robert Pack (New England University Press, 1992): "Fieldswirl"; *Poetry:* "Coming Down in Ohio" (October–November 2002), "Morning Grackles" (May 2003), "Against Blossoms" (June 2003), "Shoes" (September 2003); *Prairie Schooner:* "Edwin Muir's Palm Tree" (Fall 1994); *Sewanee Review:* "Antique German Cycle with Sidecar at Hotel du Lac," "Digging Out the Dead" (both Winter 2004), "Evening Rain and Hydrangeas" (forthcoming); *Shenandoah:* "Rodeo Poker," "Beach Beer Drive-Through" (both Fall 2004); *Southern Review:* "Lyons Den, Atlantic Avenue" (Summer 1990); *Virginia Quarterly Review:* "In the Library" (1994); *Yale Review:* "At Allen Tate's Grave" (April 1995).

LIBRARY OF CONGRESS CATALOGING-IN-PUBLICATION DATA

Smith, Dave, 1942–

Little boats, unsalvaged : poems, 1992–2004 / Dave Smith.

p. cm.

ISBN 0-8071-3105-9 (cloth : alk. paper) — ISBN 0-8071-3106-7 (pbk. : alk. paper)

I. Title.

PS3569.M5173L58 2005

811'.54—dc22   2005005122

TO *Stephen Dunn*

CONTENTS

IV

I

THE CLAM–RAKE ROOM

The maker, a man who sweats and shines as if with tears,
a tree with scars, still growls and holds the floor
where I grew up when blood startled the humid air,
stars, planets, worlds of slapped, badgered metal
spinning, clawing the dark until he tunes all
the touch of things, his groan and urge the final
grunt of play that bends me to him, watched by elders
who've sworn his rake alone scoops the bottom better.

A world of silent glare presses the sooted shop glass,
but here light's a hammer's sloped and fire-strung spit
that cuts steel to spiky fingers to rake the flesh up.
Backed to the wall, burrowed in breath, wet-eyed squint,
I'm not much, a child yet. Secrets sizzle me. He asks,
speaking through flame, *Are you the one they want?*
Those who brought me laugh, big-armed gleaners whose
hands clap at my ear with each beat sparked and splashed.

Fog so thick the cows beyond the fence slide
    in and out of focus as I follow
the dogs, the morning's metastasized ooze
    eating light, glitter's prisms.

But I find the dragons loom through dewlens
    dropped by flying spiders, each
humped, iridescent spine a living cage full
    of dreams still in bed, life

hanging off-orbit like a cat struck by a car. It's
    cattywampus, grandmother said.
She stood in the leafthick to thump it still. I
    all afternoon sat boiled by this,

until evening came cold, birdless. Then I saw
    the bull pass in pines, moonlord
of being who kept the fields whole, and I slept
    without God, away from home,

unable to answer for the guttings, lies, slicks
    of crows racketed around me.
A bare world, shivery, naked as crabapple.
    Dogs calling. Dawn's wiry walk.

THE ALTAR

Fot Sidney Burris

Once white, now blistered, scarred by stains like a sister's
scabbed legs, cheap pine with child's scrawled sun, who
hammered that one-size-fits-all step? What makes us
want to climb on wood and talk? Wobbly heart, failing
to bear some shame, my father, in silence, brought it home.

We rigged it up in our living room, shoved aside the sofa
from Sears, cleared the window to let in a better light,
pushed deeper family photos, the broken TV, jammed
our life's dropped pieces in closets. Once or twice
on it we played games dragged out, amazed and joyful

to think we might win, each keeping score like a judge.
Then, rules mattered. Gambling, rolling dice blown on
by breaths strong as heroes's we thought we could be.
Rainy days we entered the secrets of knights, queens,
quarterbacks, tycoons. When sun shone, it was waiting.

We wore a path, bored, watching at windows where
mother stepped to town in her Christmas dress, looking
past his fat chair now in the hall, her needlepoint's
red words hung by photos of their parents somewhere.
Somewhere, I said, we'd never been, and wouldn't ever go.

When it first came she asked what it was, meaning how
long must they live with this ugliness, a purple skirt,
cheap joints nobody could fix, always promising us
what hope was worth. Not much. But she, too, rose up,
voice blanket-soft, praising how families always lived,

until quiet rustled like a dog walking a floor. Sometimes
I see me singing songs he'd do to joke, whiskey-eyed,
country lovesongs, a man who's done his girl bad,
a boy peeping out of him gone before we came along.
Just words I did like him. Now I see faces stepped close,

5

their giggles, such secrets of flesh we almost forget
how the family heart flutters. Then he rose, and to us
warmed, words sobbed, hard how they shouldn't be,
so we couldn't say what was real or made up, no laughs,
just places, women's names, her eyes stilled like dice.

I saw how it was to stand on top, day bleeding dim,
a man trying to hold on, starting to howl I screwed
up, forgive me, us unsure what game we played,
what rules were, my mother's lips stiff as a girl's
the breath of a stranger's blowing over, body sagged

as in daguerreotypes at auction or flea market where
I stop to guess what each junked piece waits to say,
steps mounted, deep breath, someone's gasp when
words spill out, as always they do. I hear my mother
say no surprises, nothing's too low, nothing's too bad

the good family can't save itself. Then I see somewhere
we lived, in light pooled, before he left, the altar stripped
of books, games, news—until we'd go up, breathing
slow, starting to rock, sing, and, oh, then, their faces,
already old that summer, lifted, brimming sweetly with love.

When we went there skies flooded, curbs broached, streets
vanished, each bush and tree a survivor afloat,
an eye, heavy birds circled, red wrens, clots of finch,
robins hotelled in upper, airy rooms, the quiet so complete
you felt carried by the invisible. Uncle Brownie and Aunt Pink.

What year, place was that? My memory swims, reaches.
We'd kept them waiting, storm only context. Who
were they without me? She was dusk-tipped, powdered;
he, chocolate milk. Often acrid thick barnyard spill.
Once we peed together in the pasture, his horse wickering.

We went there, parents all in black, big words on lips,
not expecting gusts, eddies, thunder breaking the place
until all was underwater. Then we were after goats,
pigs, saving what the kitchen table's will named. Now
dawn rippled from roof tin, still rising they said, the laid-out

ones dust in heaped parlor calm. A nose I put my finger in.
One day you'll meet, they said, every voyage is for it.
I've looked, as people do, spoken. Drifts stay
wrong, some flicker through the wide gaze at me, kin
someone else would know opening doors, dark flowing past.

Then I came here, truck packed, a long life. Rains started.
Water so wretched and so wide and so high, like fear.
While we lay in our beds under slick roofs, lights
filled lanes, coiling the surface. I could think how
living must be always like them, going and coming, the wait.

Today sun. Boots on, I leashed dogs, tramped out head-bent,
looking for nothing from up there. No spatter and splash
and shake that soddens you, no plodding through clots
of weed, directionless, then gagged drains, the bodies
of small, occasional things still spinning in flow. It was all

land, giving, mucky, nose-rippling paths, root humps seen,
not tripped on, the dry-line on trunks like age, brooms
shuffling plots of broken parts we'd never mend. They
called a name I could use and return, the next corner
made a turn where I knew I'd know the way without signs.

Go on, puddles said, dogs romping, shaking like freed souls.
Then lying still as gods in the parlor where black glass
framed stars the sky seemed to throw down like rain.
A long way from Uncle Brownie and Aunt Pink.
From old bricks walked, footsteps disappearing like kisses.

VACANT LOT

For Don Johnson

Three of us, one sizzle-quick, one good hands low and loose
in center, then *whump!* the ball I'd hit already down, him

sprinting in, next turn, Lefty winding, toe hooked at burnt
scrap of two-by-four lifted from fires, a windowless house

slowly, darkly civilizing a near lot. Not this one yet, its sticky
weeds, trees I couldn't name, red thorns that raked when balls,

hard lined, fell like star rays. We'd shout hero-names, Mick,
Joe, Lefty, things we'd do days when we'd ripped past stolen

bases made of shirts, concrete sacks, bricks, local trash useful
to a dreamer's touch. Sun or spit, in dust we toiled, glory

waiting at our turns so nights we'd die imagining selves
only we could beat. Each day hardly phased lots vanished,

we blinked, struck out, homered. Above us joist-ghosts,
hammers down, howled 'Fire it, Mick,' or 'Joe's the Boy,'

or hooted Lefty's flat curve. Are they dead, veteran fathers
who lay nights dreaming themselves redeemed by sons

like Homer's sea-borne warriors gliding home? I wonder who
first dipped a shovel's lip to dice the space no evil knew?

Who chopped the trees, dug holes, moved on, who made
a ditch Lefty chucked from, my friend grenade-disarmed?

Joe, who cried to play, his wife shipped out, hasn't aged a day.
The paper's story says he held a wire where a child sizzled.

Looking up, I still find the white ball like secret joy, friends
playing with stars. Songs of urging rise from earth, except

who but fools think dirt sings? You have to stand there, dark.
I think you have to hear the fallen celebrating wars once won.

Why not say I miss my father, face above the tools,
medals, his shorts, same ties worn year after year,
the death photo, no glasses, so he seems skinned,
wise flesh? Isn't that a pretty way to put things?
Whiskers faint as my fear at the silk box, his apron,

Masonic, white as azaleas he planted below his dad's
B&O bell. Years he wooed them, and now looks up.
I stand saying I wrecked his beauty, an Alfa Romeo
roadster, white, sleek, my mother's hair blowing in it.
May next year, he'll die, oil in the street, open as a rose.

Now my time of envelopes, weekend work, the cart's
black wheels I scrub with a toothbrush, learning to pay.
I watch thick-calved women, fathers, slow walkers
who never speak, work-wearied, the wives with lists
furtive under garden signs I string. I smell them pass.

His face hangs open, the eyes drifting grass like dark
butterflies, gray pupils glazed. I wait for defeat's anger.
He's alone, digging beneath the bell, bronze god-head
on a slender pole, brass tongue silent, its rope just ivy.
Bees wheel, move on. We all pay, he says, blinking.

I watch his fingers work dirt that clings. He pushes
seed, watering what he won't see bloom. His brow's
full as the bell's honey-buds. You look like him,
they said at the funeral. I grinned, bright as undying
blossoms climbing what he'd leave, and so would I.

GENE VINCENT'S BLUE CAP

Be Bop a Lula
She's my baby

Cool March seeps from azalea beds, sun sprinkles limbs.
The blue jay's radaring head checks what I work,
his uniform quivery against the freshly clawed dirt.

Once, years back, I smelled this Spring ooze, a dirge
almost, though it doesn't sing or echo, just is.
Black leaves, green shoots, everything astir like the cool

ice-blue of Gene Vincent's cap. Three-man band, all blue.
Thirteen, date inches taller, I danced as winds do
thrashing new blossoms, and he played faster, if fast is

what you do with sax, drum, two pawned guitars, leg
fused the bus rolled, broke, cycle smashed. Susan's
father fixed him up, stitched and pinned, hence a concert

of thanks in her garage. I watched him fighting the fall
we knew he'd take, toppling among us, that bully
blue cap never lost. Be Bop a Lula again. Pain's play

makes me think of yards I raked, March, making cash
to pin on her small breast—what flower was it then?
So much we can't reclaim. His face lit when I asked

him to sign my George Washington, and now his own
blue cap lifted down, brim gilded like Odysseus,'
scratching *Gene Vincent! Be Bop a Lula.* I hear the cop

spit who dragged him from oily dark, who gassed the nurse
who said *Do you know who this boy is?* Just another noise,
I think, night's piece of ice in the rake's teeth breaks, yet here

in the yard all at once I'm dancing, girl's hand in mine, dirt's
slick, daffodils rising. I'm shaking it up inside, I'm
certain life's worth it all, Gene plays, you're my baby, yeah.

BEACH BEER DRIVE-THROUGH

Nags Head, North Carolina

A shop for needs and thirsts. One lane. Surf a fuse
of white where the eye rolls straight through,
sea that gray of aircraft carriers and small tenders.
Along the sand go ladies, gusting summer dresses,
some with wheeled carts full of children, others
bikinied, striding hard, as if a debt is coming due.

Dawdlers in motion, motiveless, family, crowds
must be imagined, the furniture of someone's stage,
entries, exits. They have their story: what you
wanted, that new name, the past, even the past's shrewd
understanding why, tight-lipped, they stare at blue
far out where nothing is, some laughing, some in rage.

They're no different from two looming in silhouette
where beer's stacked in fake snow, flat selves about
to be a merchant's heart attack, a surprise proposal.
They are the thing you can't escape; they make art.
That way one of them holds a sun-fired pistol.
That way one of them looks like home falling down.

If you'd had the dysentery of uncles, so weak hour after hour
you'd lay fallen like a bird's broken wingblade, but enough
juice to flutter when our coach cried "Up!" and then croak
to the bastard a quick "fuck you and your grandmother,"
you'd know the kind he was. And if his stubbled face hung
when you walked past the pine box, if you'd think to ask why

its ridges and cracks looked like hurt, and rain spit in his eyes
to make that barn-owl black and faint flicker you might argue
was only man's sin passing out of them, he'd as soon have
kneeled down on bleeding Christ as given you his name. So,
what would it help if I said I've carried this teammate years
in my head? I'd like to forget, to blink off his skin bloodied,

chicken-bone legs all yellowed, bent flapping, and cast-off
canvas football pants not fit for jvs in a knot, and that helmet
exploded as cut-blocked, rolled, battered he bounced up
retching and cursing, "Lord fuck you, buddy!" little fist-bud
grazing my nose like a bee. But I can't, and no good reason,
the way a gift, a word holds you right there. Just breathing.

The way, pads flung aside, stink in the showers, chest puffed
with pink, girlish veins, bruises the blue of lingerie, he saw
me bend, giggle at butt-burn scars worming in locker room
light's fluorescence, maybe doing a scoliatic walk he had,
wobbly as a duck-footed whore. Lucky, our parents said,
you're not him, poor boy without mother or man to lean on,

just tin trailer wind rattles as he sleeps. Here's to the shade
who tackled a tank to fight for fat boys at home on fat wallets,
who we called "Can of Beans," arms flapping, who zigged
our yards with razzy mowers, who threw balls to our dogs,
carried dogs to our vets, nailed and painted and caulked us,
and never said anyone set up a play to get him punched flat

or put the last dump of the day in his shoe while he toweled off.
Can, is it shame makes me miss you when I see how crazy
your truck looks up a tree in the news and nowhere your face?
Or how the runt of the litter looks after it's been raised up,
and by God it's ours, every mark's there, shape and color, it
won't whine or shiver or back off and, goddamn, it will hunt,

it will howl when dark moves, teeth flash too, and those ears
lay back, if cornered, for it knows what happened before.
Weeks ago I asked why you came back after the war and you
snarled, "Where the fuck should I go, Bud?" Somewhere
good, I'd like to say I said, where home isn't all we get
screwed by, sucked into, and can't give up or stop dying for,

but wisdom wasn't our long suit, as you knew, and no sense
of selfish pain makes me speak. It's only remembering
a long-past moment when, naked, you slapped me. Words
barked, blood on cold tile as we fought, coaches laughing.
I knew I'd hold your face beaten to hell, no win, no loss,
just rebuke for what it named, buddy, and it's all I have now.

When we were done she said it burned. Love can, I said,
hearing the push and pull of hours, the years grind.
The girl, a guy's wife in Pittsburgh, red dress on toilet door,
made a noise in her throat, soft, but ugly all the same.
Face pale, underwear glowing on chair, soul in a hurry,
dusk shivering down on buds, azaleas, jonquils, tulips.
I was happy, Cumberland left behind. No, she said, I mean
you've torn me, I wasn't ready. Don't you know anything yet?

Be always ready, I knew what those words hurried to mean.
I'd told her I drove train diesels. I watched one in my head
tearing the darkness, not caring what came next. But
I felt my legs start to burn like they did tucked up
so I could lean way out of the cab as it climbed.
I felt her knees bumping mine under the sheets.
Rain came, brittle at the window, then quiet, thickening.
I was afraid to touch her again, I said what do you mean?

The usual thing, a man won't wait, afraid of the dark.
You can't help it, pushing, taking it too fast, not seeing.
I kept hearing the way she said *a man*. Off in the yard,
a diesel's horn wailed, its B&O face pinched, light
swelling bigger, speed balling to weight I couldn't feel,
somebody inside, I knew, squinting at blurred signals,
looking for mistakes. My job was to see into that dark.

Don't rush, my father said, take time, go easy, come back.
Nothing terrible had hurt me yet, my lunch tin was full,
thermos wet with whiskey, streets shining below,
late dawn snow somewhere ahead. Hungry, I'd eat,
lean out of my cab, coffee churned to burning flecks
on my skin when curves came. I might think about her.
I wouldn't fail, brakes would hold the dark off. No problem.

Ahead of me the bump and shriek of the B&O's couplings.
Coal ash now on green lawns. I smelled roses in her hair.
You don't know so much, she said. *A man*. She said that, too.

At cross-hung street wires we stop, someone's pickup,
scorched pieces in the road, fire's odor, a dead man
covered by a sheet, boots out, flares fizzing, fear
like electric fuse in the heart alive, uncaught,
going on. Night's faces in car windows beside us

flushed, flickering, wordless. Swinging on the curve's
edge one Fall night summery with linger of heat,
I felt once how little it takes, oblique and unseen,
to send us skidding, and my white Chevrolet,
flying home, suddenly was ditch-deep. Midnight,

you and I crawled into sky-fire of piled-up peanut husks,
on stubble-shaved ground not alone, wrong enough
in our sight even bourbon's spidering haze was
not enough to explain what we saw. Dazed, we
slid as if from a noon horror matinee to dark safe

with each sleepy tree, house, parked car. No evil clawed
behind us, life stale as popcorn. And if in that field
would rise Cape Cods, toys, trailered boats, now
came the hiss of leaf-fall, and husk rustle,
and faces like bats flicking night, whoever saw.

Big men, white-sheeted, stood, eyes to the flame-ooze,
smoke's stream starring wood's crown and tin
roof where a farmer lived. Sky heaved
its black down thick like hatred we hid in,
half breathing. We smelled it, we licked it, we felt

fire push us in night's room. Now, on starred glass,
going ahead, I see again how easy a body hangs,
puffed and pillowy, a man blazing, that one gulp
of gasoline its life, then black into black.
We crawled, bellying by cinders, unharmed, or so

17

we tell it, if asked, safe forty years, the wry hallelujahs
like cheers when you wake in nightmare from booze,
friends who might lean down weirdly to ask *You
ok?* Their faces, eye-holed in white, were moons
above ditch edge, at road's berm where we will not

twine again, thrusting, drinking moon brew, blanket on
that black spot following the cross, flames, voices
bubbling at wreckage, our radio's faithful choir
of hearts—James Brown, Chuck Berry, Elvis—
as if trying to climb free to the stars singing on, but

we were running, not able yet to say what we had heard,
not yet remembering fear and flames that always come
unlooked for, not knowing all we can do is wait
until we cannot, then shouting *Bastards!*, stopped
where feet tap forward, wanting out of light's sizzle again.

OYSTER BEDS

On the marriage of Lael and Hunter Eley

Wicked, I called them, ridged shells soft-folded, tide-shifters,
clingers to white dull walls of homes I could never live in, so

I thought. Then slipped among the inner rooms of shells, heaps,
pier-holders, little joists, sepulchral cities of families, quiet's

blizzards of tiny fish, too, feeling's shapes, edge schools
that pump and nudge and woo the eye that falls upon them.

These seemed easy to understand, crowds of dreamers in blue.
But I had no taste for what dark gouged, slurped, raked, beds

of lumps like saltwater foam some god commanded to be flesh.
I knew what they were. One in summer light opened on me.

Where it lay in water's bed, sunning, I walked, not warned.
Then the white of bone slipped out, my foot's blood flowed,

teased stain of me large, mysterious, that left on us surrounding
touch like a first kiss. Mud shone as if torched that day. Skins

of sails cut the harbor to a room, bobbers left shoes, watches,
rings, near-naked in light, walking sand, knee-deep flirting it.

For you I'd gone forth. Now I heard old words: come on, heart,
give the thing your try, blest are willed-together ones, sweeter

opening, and chillest tides strike seed. I walked swallowing in
your uplifted loving face, by marsh and hill, lying nights alive,

rivulets of salt scaling us, life's mouth wide. We knew it. Gulp,
you said, it's good. We would eat, be whole together, then rise up.

LYONS DEN, ATLANTIC AVENUE

Virginia Beach, Virginia

What happened to years? What room key with no lock,
what match-pack lies in desk drawer my hand rummages again?

To her bar-stool I came, hoped the girl waiting tables
would want me, dropped fists of dollars for dark bottles, heard

the jukebox croon everybody loves somebody. But who did?
Coins rose to her fingers as faces slashed cheek to eye,

or just sorrow gouged, got still, and some went to alleys
to brawl, and some bought me beer. Boy wonder, said one

of the Navy Yard's finest, say again what you do? I watch
the angel work her tables, I'd say, and it was always good

enough, so he'd watch, too, Creole, shark-wide eyes,
calves and tits of a runner, would dip for a spray of change,

two-step for tips, skin smell like doughnuts, we said, brown
legs long, short skirt. *What you want, sweets?* Love'll do,

I said. Her lips, at match-flare, said *Fuck you!* Shoulders
like wings, she spun to the palms of others. I'd drink, think

of Penny Lane, Beatles, love's funny pain. *Who'll love me
now?* she'd sing. We'd know not us, but the legless dude

fatigued like he'd been to Nam, body-board knuckled up,
begging till coins showered, then closing, drunks, brawlers,

ghosts gone, her, me moping tables. She'd do it, then,
whatever he wanted, put it out, him eating love itself,

gumbo and eggs, mayonnaise sandwich, Bud iced
so fog lathered it. Singing, washing mugs while he chewed,

she'd nudge me, *Go,* cottonmouth-quivery. What the hell
is love? I'd ask her, but no answer, so I shove hand in drawer,

touch box musky with beads long off string, there it is,
under old checks, note paper-clipped tight saying *Sweetie,*

it's baaed, not good! Sing-song, too, in my ear where
her patron placed his fist, snarling *Asshole!* as she laid one

steak-knife where he wouldn't like it. Reach, touch all,
since night's still coming on time. Maybe somewhere she's

singing *My Sweetie don't love me no more.* Listen. It's him
wheeling in with that little gas torch he used to light her

up, that flesh she'd sell for his bottle, who's maybe dead
(Don't ask, don't beg, son, never. Love'll dance like a dog.)

Yellow moon over ocean, home she'd be pushing
him past moth-hum. Think *love.* In his tub, he'd sleep,

she'd wash, breasts swinging, Jagger on; smoke, screams.
She'd lay folded in ash like trash in the alley. What is love

that can't be killed if it bites and rattles? Stick head in
the Lyons Den door, call out his name, listen to feet slap-slap,

that waiting, dark, like a moth bulb-scorched, you see
her same eyes, and his name like a fist, logical as a six-pack.

Or open the match-pack you drop back in a drawer, let it
flare, chewing at light. No cost. Cup palms, too, for the time

that's left, dump it in the box where rooms live and worse
people gasp in dreams you can't stop having. She's there,

love's only answer. If now she says *Turn the light out,*
I'm not what I once was—nod, act as if you've nothing to ask.

Pure, Casteen's big blue letters said, *Pure.* My date cried
stop, she needed *it,* midnight near, and I was pumped,
thinking I'd touch *it* at last, the old story. She floats up
on the black slick of that past, poised, darts to the Ladies.

The night feels manic. I try to see what road to park, where
it will happen that I can't remember, but *it* must be
under that cheerleader's white skirt, *it* that makes yes
when her legs go flying over the game bench where I sit

hunched in pads, unsalted, waiting, and she says *I want it,*
meaning little dark rooms, maybe more. Is *it* in me?
What if I'm wrong? I dial for tunes and Sunday comes,
the preacher crows *it*'s a mistake, but God gives *it,* is *it,*

so I see I don't know what *it* is that itches all over me.
Then a stoplight flashes, two cars nosing side by side.
Is everything predictable but the girl from my home room,
shirt lifted, small breasts brilliant at glass, saying here *it* is?

If I think of those days, *it*'s a story with no start, no end.
Even when I go with the dead I'll see her nipples flare
like Cadillac taillights, like Christmas packages of *it,*
like the feeling when you rise from *its* body, and glow.

We all saw *it,* three ex-GIs in the station, their sucked
Marlboros hanging while they waited, Korea's silk
shirts and Hank Williams sagging all over each one.
Then on oil-filthy floors she broke past their shadow,

and, whether God's or mine, whatever *it* was she made ready,
that was the year I watched a parking lot of night's floaters
like children, I saw the wheels smoke for joy. I did not
yet know these particulars meant little. I did not see them

blow up the condom, or set *it* fizzing like love in that gassy
perfume she sprayed at the *Pure* Station. I only report *it,*
eyes liquid, drained glancing faces, and divorce statistics
say three of four die unredeemed, no matter what *it* comes to.

II

" . . . a hilly peninsula in the middle of Lake Como
in the foothills of the Italian Alps"
Bellagio Study and Conference Center

Groggy souls just arrived at Milan's airport, we
wave to a sad-eyed native holding our name.
I ask where we go, but he won't say, driving
a black Mercedes that clings around curves
like a possum in Maryland's night wood where
my dead uncle took me hunting. I remember
eyes in the flashlight's beam, stars above trees.
So, like a child, I ask again. The man shrugs.
Maybe he doesn't understand it's language
I want for the mountains around us, black walls
plunging to what must be Lake Lecco, my map
revealing a paradise of deep, purest blue.
No stars yet, this early dusk, pink hazy light
like a woman's slip pooled on bone-tile floor.
Will it be a kind of resort, secluded, erotic?
I speak more slowly to touch his lost Italian
understanding, but only the big, sliding wheel
hisses back and the plush carriage we're in
swoops old road as if we're tracked. My wife
grins, nods. I've been reading of writers, wars,
Hemingway, who played with women here,
so I whisper to her "death in the afternoon."
She only sighs at whisked-by oleander, white
bursts, and gasps of wisteria gating poles over
roses like blood veins. Sun butters our thighs.
Paradise, we say, like a prayer, over and over,
and everything here is perfect, road rising
ever gently, his driving buoyant at cliffs so
deep the drops open our mouths in fear. Then
the Villa Serbelloni appears, the residence
awarded to people who dream. Our bags
land neat on the grass, ethereal hostess waits,
engine idles, birds sing. Then, from his wheel,
he calls out "Pre-Alps," in movie Italian,
"What comes-a before real thing, Signor,
life before-a poem." Mirrored by his glass,

dead-pan, I watch him start back for others
until he sinks to gorges and shadows, losing
the living path that snakes from Bellagio
to the world. Ahead of us the Villa's rooms
blank and clean where bats swirl quietly out.

SEEKING WORDS

a wolf's head under the pillow will secure sleep . . .
—SEXTUS PLACITUS, *Medicinia de Quadrupedibus*

Night clouds roll across the Lake's floor and blur
granite slopes of the Alps I imagine
men climb, one foot after another. Slowly,
down-spiraling stars vanish as I see them
over Virginia's marshes. My grandfather
said God seems to call them back. House dark,
that wind his robe-sweep as he searched for light.

Writing, I feel the step of fear in the first
storm-flash, and blackness we scramble to see.
Below, tile roofs, walks, trees hiss each instant
lightning quivers like fate, then absence
deeper than dream or knowledge can say.
Travelers, we own no candle, match, or words
local enough to name what wakes each alone.

Even late-shift survivors, sleep brick-weight,
shake, rise, drift—watching the wrack come on.
We don't know which world we're in, the wicked
thrash of nightmare's fall or float of time's keep.
In black rooms we cup hands to make a light.
Dunn's poem says, like marsh reed's scrape,
"I haven't chosen to be alone but am."

As we are. Hours of wind-howl, all dark-tongued.
Then haze, silvery ropes hung like the mind's
cast for the unseen. Quiet on stone-notch, grass,
road-rut, bridge-brace. Soon footsteps. Each drop
trembles, shapes, falls, skitters away. Rough sun
rolls ahead, coming on. All now look and blink,
the slink of words turning to shadows as if chased.

What should we call them, shy visions, storm-bent,
who seem hurt creatures in cupped hands of walkers?
Ours at home are green, pink-throats, quick eyes.
These are the size of cigarillos, brown of Army tents.

Male and heavy-lidded, blending equally in
where lichen weaves to cement ages of dried soil,
monastic rock that's robed in thick ropes of grape.
Everything here attaches itself (say sloughed skins)

to rough, barely grippable bulge and slope of stone's
muscle, so you get the idea there must be something
way down, savage, inside that all winds its way
toward, magnetic but shy, a turn that heads tune

to at least swish of uphill winds. Chuteless tiny
hang-gliders who work a leaf edge, their ancestry's
moral tides, rank debris of fate. I admire each
little skitterer with rock-claws fixed to trees.

We find their Roman noses pointed to blue space
that laps polluted lakes, as if they wait, having been
told great love will move mountains. But our step
suffices, like thundery weight, to send them straight

back inside to cling where oldest dark cools
crevice and flitch; yet always out come one or two,
tail-nipped, slow, looking for the lesson of the day.
In shorts and tourists' floral T-shirts we stoop

and lift the hedge of pruned green: there they are,
the elders, pale, some rose-scented, some pine twigs.
Palms out we try to lure one, but she sticks tight,
tonguing the air, eyeballing, wanting no offer

but breath, stone, a day where she may end outlined
like crochet imprints they've got in the gift shops.
Her skeleton flames with sun the mountain drowns
her in two hours each day. Saints, so glory-primed

their oily eyes only blink when we cast the end
with two boomer handclaps, even this can't shake
them from the trance-work of the near invisible,
stolid watchers of something too big for us to name.

CONFESSION

Is it that it's hard to know how much to tell,
or what to tell, or what we do not know, the unwritten?

Here, the "cinnamon" (who named this tree that?) spruce
seems solid as a sergeant watching drill, yet lacy
green keeps off the hardest rain. I watch
people standing, looking as if they have been numbed.

Nazis came here once, uniforms dramatic black,
the lightning insignias silver as moonlight
flashed from the lips of brandy glasses.
Laughing girls lightly touched their sleeves.

Down passes shadow-dappled the 88s would begin.
A boy from Norfolk swelled up, a village dog
chewed what had been neck, gulped an eye.

Was it a shell's wind that lifted him like a swift?
Or a mine behind a tree where modestly he went?

Now I tell you my tale of love gone bad,
the little tug at heart you faintly remember,
though it's only an idea, and the fräulein
lying in the moon that seems so different now.

Perhaps you were her first. Those breasts like eyes.
The pubic openness, that foreign thing.

So like the boy they will find,
those black clad, motor rumbling, who
drive on thinking they'll never think of this,
white handkerchiefs wiping the glasses they wear.

Pounding, bullying, dull ratchet-sound, big tracks,
earth-mover, some kind of dozer clank past
where I sit listening to cicadas tear apart
cooling summer's shudder. Something big bashes

the olives, tread slops along the hillside crushing
footsteps we left last night, daily work done.
Up there pale arms barely hold on, grim wheel
alive to each of earth's curves, the villas struck

by the grip of gross treads, swivel of old grease.
Sounds deep nerves once made for other men
long gone, fields of fire, redoubts their purpose,
opening a way to pass alive through dreams.

Or at least by slopes carved to hold the weight
Allied planes ungathered in silk chutes,
some hung swaying to inner notes. The dead's
stubborn signature roars and retreats like our fate.

He'll push on, not knowing my work. I don't ask,
like philosophers pacing, what life wants,
or why some men can't stand quiet rooms.
I don't listen to learn how this passage breaks

the dripping pump where a bucket hangs, flings
bats like defective stars out at dusk, and lifts
the leathery face at the stove, all day cooking,
sure garlic's needed, and something dark in song.

It's what will go around me when walls fail,
the house voice saying no, no, no. "What was that?"
"Nothing," she says, a face I once ached for.
As if it had just called my name, afraid and old.

Voices climb the hill, weaving through olive trees
laden with old men who pluck bags of fruit, passing
cool stone steps, arches of white buds, straight up
high walls even a medieval catapult could not breach.
Greased, squeaking, bodies bared for playful diving,

the slim girls I see dockside at dawn, toes bright
with silver rings and pink paint, gold chains at necks,
cigarillos they smoke like tiny eels swimming the air.
They laugh at the night, the love they have made.
Above boats heavy men hum. I can see them glisten.

Soon, the boat's bow glides out, a dog sniffing wind.
When it turns, the hull is a ferry to invisible shores.
From the window where I write I see an old body
go in like a pour of grappa, feel a sweetness that takes
each into the deeps marked *No swimming. Bad Waters.*

Rain spatters slick cobblestones where walked God
only knows how many, as my grandmother would say.
Through tall windows I watch haze take the east pass,
owning mountains the way Nazis did with panzers,
that loud clanking and chinking forward only thumps
of lightning's concussions, all life hidden in shadows.
What else is war but cold hunks of metal, emptied
of malice, crews off in cafés, boys boasting of evils
they might do if the officers would ever go to sleep?

Here, in paradise of oleander, peonies, roses, high air
makes it easy to dream, as they must have, men given
back after the stinky columns squeezed through veins
of raw rock, one in the café reading the news, pale
as philosophers and poets with villas once, nights
beating hard down on Lecco and Como and nothing
could breach that serene lap of lake's wave on wave.
Predictable as the family. The way I used to feel
nights rain skittered down my grandmother's tin roof.

Ticked glass, everything sluiced fresh, sizzling onto
the petals of her prized hydrangeas. That's what comes
back now, the blue surprise when you'd touch one,
shaking so much wet on you and the dark spots then,
and the look she'd have when she'd see you walking in,
puzzled, same look the day my uncle dragged home alive,
himself stiff as canvas tents, his combat knife so sharp
he might have shaved someone deep, a boy who liked
throwing it at black pine until, bored, he sold it to me.

I remember how it rusted, left out in the workshed,
with the spats, the web-belt canteen, the empty holster
and the opera ticket with the photo of an unknown girl
whose eyes were my grandmother's when she lay in rain.
Summer nights she'd smell the hydrangeas, say she knew

the boy would come home, things would be the same.
She'd cry. Then he *was* home. Then it was dark all over.
The way it is tonight, rain shaking Bellagio's hydrangeas.

When we asked, they said you never came here, silent
crawler long banished from wayside bricks and tunnels,
self-preserver hied away from grotto lawns, feeder on
whatever the high rocks keep, drinker of clouds. Yet
soles landed quiet as we climb to where Pliny lived,
we watch the whipped ripple of your passage, the back
of your head splays in the sun, swaying to see who we are.

Respecters of vision, we kneel, remove hats, Ray-Bans,
lower our brows, smell what tourists have trampled.
Faint birdsong prays at cliffs cool over Lake Lecco,
our minds emptied of colors or names like you. But
the mile-deep blue of the ancient water flashes, boats
tick zigzag routes with certain purpose we do not have.
Looking up we could not see this garden, cool and dark,

distant as time's heart. We did not expect you to be
still here, in our age, where the gods, having lunch,
explained the order of fields, streets, entrails, crops
revealing secrets, each thing bearing its difficult word
of prophecy. Who came first, before beer cans tossed
beside your self-canceling sleeve of transparent skin?
How many watched you this way, waiting? What name

after our cramps, sweat, long climb down, do we offer?
Yes, we will tell them, when they ask, the hard faces
who bring us platters of fish and meat and gold rice,
their sweets from stone cellars, earth's finest wine.
They will want markers, step-count, warning: we say
stones, grapevine, human trash, footprints, the pulse
of water like redemption. One of you is there, in pieces.

Flat green from handlebar to bloomed skirt of sidecar,
no chrome, fat wide seat fit for Nazi corporal who
wore gold wings like Mercury's on his black outfit,
this machine, parked on cobblestones, brings back war
I know only from Hogan's Heroes, Lee Marvin, dates,
tests failed. I drink, watch the young waitress, daydream.

Roses plush, pink as a village girl's lips line a terrace
where thousands of years wear down to the lake's edge,
its blue-black depth a kind of vile perfection I cannot
penetrate wherever I stand. Boxwoods, trimmed, round,
thicken like hair on a Jew's boy in market stalls; plump
oleander trees, whiter than a German lieutenant's gloves

drop tender offerings on unmeasurable dark with each
gust of the coming storm. Where can they go, cupped
blossoms, prim as small frocks, when fish come grazing?
I see them spin as if they were wish-thin ravioli nosed
by black-tipped and gold-scalloped cruisers, gone when
rain spatters wine-burdened tables, a child's wet mouth.

How easy it is to see the sun reaching down, that slips
under that day's barely breathing girl, and strokes, deft
finger of the glittering officer still grayed with boot polish,
a lesson from his father, sliding back, forth until it is done.
Day after day, why should she scream? Do the stones care?
Then dinner in the rock grotto, her blinkless eyes, a shine

on his boots she remarks over potato soup, a fine leather,
almost edible cooked right. Surviving, she sips, waits,
feels under table lace his feet come, a shape like panzers.
Tonight's cyclist will leave her, a room in the Serbelloni.
Their clothes hung over chairs like dreamers who visit,
asleep, bed, water shimmering. Who would know, a war on.

John departs for his studio, its walls circular as prayer,
lined with images of his father for the animated movie afoot
where the mob loans him, then owns him; then John erases or
he can't invent the next panel and there the wall is white as sky.

I walk to my room tucked in a high corner like a garret,
my computer humming for the words it expects from me,
all others doing the same, breakfast, soft talk behind us now.
In the big hall a gathering of Jews and Arabs, a mini-conference,

locks its doors, long tables, babble of shouts, waiters in, out.
Planning what to do with Jerusalem when war's finished, they
sound like the Harvard man and the Michigan lesbian at tennis
on the terrace, clay dust old as Rome heeled up, fat ideas lunging,

blows couched in ritual courtesy, players with little to lose.
"Great shot." "Yours, too." Thunk and answering ca-thunk
like remote mortars I can't see, only the crystalline blue lake
and infinite buttery sun I imagine those inside are bartering for.

Those who win or lose don't come here, they are still
washing clothes in a ditch, running checkpoints to steal food,
holding their breath as they pee quietly over the planted mine.
I try to see them with three servants per meal, naps, discussions,

but it's John's father I see, Italian, in debt, wiped out.
Below, an army of workers moves at hill's bottom, quiet
so valuable here, they ply simple tools of their fathers, silent
snippers, mowers, diggers in glare's boil. Rows of olive trees

tremble with speckled leaves as they advance. One, two
voices call, faces lift here, there as if to see what is waiting.
Hawks, small-beaked, orbit and swoop, held off by glints of
sparrows working hard over nests, mouths open, hot day ahead.

I can see from my room dark streets of Bellagio spool
maze-like to Lake Como's gelato shops, family boats, ferries,
the Villa's day workers who sit, eyes black, as we make words
we pretend will sing to our neighbors, friends, even gray fathers

sailing home desperate, wordless. It's like movies here,
old, close, shocking, the way we find, astonished, a perfectly
preserved Nazi cycle and sidecar. In an alley we stare as John
buys us drinks. We praise his work. Jews, Arabs silently file by.

LAST SUPPER

i.m. David Corson

We walk out on the terrace, hills plummet,
Lake Como black under man-made floors
that hold us over Pliny's lost orchard.
Bats skitter, swoop, savor small
delicacies we do not see, bottomless
water alive with moonlight like rumors
of joy beyond the last night. We're ghosts

standing, rich drinks, ideas that hum.
Words sewing like bees in roses,
we feel body heat's swirl, and star-chill.
We tremble, new friends, the night's
fish, wine—Colli de Luni Rosso?—
Italian fruits sweet on fingers,
remembering our days not yet past.

Then grappa, your toast, Australian, sly,
archaeologist's jargon, and Latin
names, sanctuaries we walked, wiping
some saint's cloth at your brow,
bending closer, acolyte to the dead.
Is this Paradise? you joked. Ta-dum.
Our grins don't answer you anymore

or find, below, hidden by night's stones,
voices of girls, faint, razzing
scooter uphill, their song plunging.
"They won't hold us tonight, ah,
no warm lips, just cold lake wind,"
our fake Motown made you laugh.
Then you slipped off like the snake
crossing our path, a shadow's whirlpool

all that stayed where the lake waited.
The day before the last a rich man

tried to berth his boat there,
but failed coming about, boom
spinning, giddy girlish laughter all
swarming us as we typed. No room
for snake and man and girl, you jibed.

The invisible. We waved and gestured,
ready to fly home, full of the unseen,
the unsaid. Soft words going in.
Then a bat dipped close, like a girl's
thigh flashed. It's that, I said. You
turned, not coughing yet, tongue quick.

Poetry you mean?

MILAN CATHEDRAL ECLIPSE

For Dee

We went that last day, time running out, agreed
when it grew dark to make love. How long
we'd been lost we didn't know until the train
climbed the lake's ridge, our words the old ones,
alien in this Italian sun, lovers flying where
we heard the dark was making. Who knew
if we'd gone wrong? From Milan's Bauhaus
station we trudged in gritty light, asking faces.
Gothic spires tall, dimly cool, Cathedral spiked,
leering gargoyles. I felt bad years fall away.
I wanted to find you in our first room, married.
We rode a lift, then steps, then stone tunnels
well-lit, going up fast like braced lawyers,
stepping out. Girls on blankets, beached, Cokes,
guys fisting bags of chips, a few flared eyes
full of fear like the aged have. I had to look
at roofs like teeth below. Stone beasts, grim
as lust, clawed through walls hung with light,
unseen by boys sailing frisbees; boomboxes
barked, nuns snoozed. No dark for us anywhere.
How did Italians do it? Priests panhandled
water bottles, bowing, praise everywhere.
I saw a slight grayness once, a movement
like trees, no soundless room, no closet even,
no dizzying, chest-grabbing Puritan blackout.
When a girl, topless, flashed Ray-Bans at me
I turned in retreat like a saint for a door.
Then a blonde, all legs, snapped us in light
so buttery our heads went haloed, the glittery
cell phone towers of Milan hung like a past
no longer ringing us. Why so glum? You teased
as I slumped, oozed out where the piazza's
touristy lens-crowd flashed madly, as if
we were famous flames lighting them up.
Little left but pews, naves, nooks to kneel in,

or this sacred light so famous Italians sell it.
Have a little faith, you whispered. The sky
glowed like ice. We kissed, then, in a cab.
Our plane, huge, hollow as a chapel, hissed
us up toward where home waited, then dark
locked us down. Rows of empty seats, just
a handful of priests snoring airline wine.
I said "We can't get any higher than this,"
as we lapped the free liquor. Sidereal
as love, the plane's oval glasses starred,
you led me where it was lightless, way back.
I remember the wings. I remember the sea's
black, and your face the only glow alive.
Then wheels rolled us forth. Dawn. A priest
rose, joking 'first light, then dark, then light.'
Shades on, we descended, blinked, greeting all
with words we knew. Soon it would get dark again.

III

Beneath leaf-light fluttered ceilings,
river's gaudy flashes and streams,
language lost when we waken
in books, their muted horizons,

I step quietly. Five students sprawl.
Two at bookbags curled, fetal.
Three appear almost bags of flesh,
shot in chairs, or robbed, trashed,

mysteries unsolved. But no crime,
though something's come
to rake loot as students sleep.
Some treasure seems missing, its feel

bleeds under these sleepers. I take
my chair, and sigh, break my book,
and one's cell phone rings like hope
uselessly. Brave enough to flop,

they drift past tests dim as water.
What makes them dream? I feared
unknowns, gaps, history's blank
with no name, no clue. Panicked,

I'm their age again, unsure, then
asleep, watching my head lift in
nightmares of who I am, or not.
1965. Ratty jeans, no socks,

button-down, tweed, striped tie
half-loose, hair chaos like JFK.
Puppies, we crawled to the edge,
night barked big words, little dogs

of Cuba. What did we know?
Some died. Asia. Some I knew.
Notes on dates, facts, forces,
theorems, theories, abstract choices,

battles, weapons ... what explained?
Did dead fathers find it this way,
in books, sleeping? I'm vexed,
a teacher wandering dusty stacks,

as I often do, my ache to read
less than trouble on my mind,
a need to loaf as light twists
leaves, drops here. Is it happiness

flows by, like sun on water?
What I feel with these dreamers,
faces blank of intent,
earphones on, plays the end

of songs to me foreign as tombs,
books they won't open or use
to sniff blood's secrets, facts
somebody's listed, names, lost

hopes surfaced here again
and again. Let tests be done.
My heart's up, down. These
go steady as new machines.

Each will go fast, faster. Then stop.
Still as memory. Slack as rope.
Books gape. The mystery's
breath itself, sun, dark. Sharp keys

poke my pocket like a need.
Still, I don't want to leave.
Lingering with penitents
soon to wake seems mostly right,

if it's little, really, but masks,
a room of dust on fate's books,
a room of sun blurring words
where people come for answers.

I saw him stand where sun seemed like a girl's grin.
Nervous, I said I liked a book he was in.
A New Life. His first novel—only I poisoned
his day, he lashed out. "I wasn't that man!"
Fine with me, I backed off. I still like the book.
Malamud's been dead years but better luck
for his hero, a man of words this man assembled.
A patient man, fastidious, but no saint or angel.
Otherwise, how could he know what the world is?
His tales had edges, thorns, knots, worries because
they wanted to say why that man put on those pants.
I remember him short like a cowboy, bald, slight,
and pale as frogs by the Bennington College ponds.
He walked alone. He watched how the night bends
black over every shape—but I don't think he saw
the sublime the world abundantly offers, only the sore
sufferings of men he ached not to chronicle,
and did, and love's craziest ends he dwelt
most lordly upon. Who else mated a woman
and a chimp in a clever rabbinical novel? Then
set out to document the history of amour in the west?
He adored to touch women, though purely. Perhaps
as fondler one of the older kind, gentle, his books
fixing them like butterflies in a glass box;
women unlike men, lacking decay's smell, unused.
Remember the parties, quiet as interviews at his house?
His eyes had that frog-weep of pond-dwellers, a grim
staring nose-to-chest he'd give, like a scrape you were in.
You'd look away, wonder how anyone took his glare.
He'd talk fast, getting hot. You might feel tears.
He'd bitch, he'd bristle. Making life made him impatient.
Slender volumes, half-priced, the just, unjust, fated.

EDWIN MUIR'S PALM TREE

St. Andrews, Scotland

Secluded in slate courtyard that faces inward from slap
of the North Sea, where he lived, husband, shadow.
Muir's palm tree, Douglas Dunn says, its fronds
hissing, clacking like small swords in the least swat
of winds across walls and cheeks. Not leaves,
poor nest-makers, root-bound. No fruit.
A fierce beauty left, passionate as the poet

writing alone on sea-gust nights. The withering age
which it remarks seems still wind-skids,
a cluster-bomb of ice that fragments and sticks
blade-tips, twists, and springs cat-like
in the clutch of Muir's love. Today I hear
Danes clamber shale-face and grip ledge
of earth, hot breaths. The palm hisses how they shored

themselves here—rapists, worse—the axe-men
soon old enough to be pointed out by children,
hairy aliens in long pale light, the last
squatting to pee, oblivious, kin refusing him,
blotched skin, songs broken hard
on tongue that still can say lost words.
Feathers swirled, a small gull grabs slick stone

as Muir's palm scratches slate. My mouth's brine,
mist fogs glass where he once watched rain run.
What good is such green in such cold?
Some lives, driven shoreward by night fires,
go wilding, swaying in sexy midnight light.
These fronds are horses stamping exile ground.
Wind's honed stalks his salt-breaths tuned to lines.

AT ALLEN TATE'S GRAVE

Sewanee, Tennessee

Tate lies in the dark, green ground
where sun shines enough to sift
holly's thick, inflexible limbs.
They claw a man who pushes round
to come mourning, one not quick

to see what looms, whips, or hangs
in summer's raking heat. Winters,
leaf-naked, it's easier to review
what nature thinks, avoid stings,
step over sleeping copperheads, move

unburdened by sore cause on tongue.
Cardinals summer here. They boom
their grave speech at meadowlark,
finch, wren, fearless of anyone
almost, blood spots from the heart

of the sky that daily sinks to dark.
The mystery is what loves a man.
Writers come here; they look, leave.
A cheerful gray squirrel barks.
The stream mumbles, as if it grieves.

Every Spring turns predictable.
The botany class studies dogwood,
musicians play airs, half-reached tunes.
Some hearts (yours!) stir with zeal.
Noon broods. Then it's afternoon.

WARREN'S FLOWERS

West Wardsboro, Vermont

Out of the chalet, chests warm with bourbon
poured lunch long, we moved in leaves
Vermont lay down season after season,
going to the pond Warren dammed up,
where each lap, he said, sounded a line
he strung over the water, over blackness
it made my skin creep to look down upon.

But now I saw his writing room out there
under the great canopy where the sun
occasionally starred the resolute dark,
its walls only screen, the roof flat,
sloped like a face nothing here loved.
As if some interrogation was in progress,
in the middle sat a plain desk and a chair.

Blossoms white as camellias, some fat
like magnolias, budded the understory,
emerging from the earth no one had
disturbed with plow or foundation,
fecund as answers. Already we had come
to log-steps he hacked in the hillside,
crows jeered our intrusion, a web's flap

grazed my face. Things moved. I'd been in
the pond already, the slick newts eyeing me,
the moss that clung like unsloughed skin,
a bottom no weight could hold long on.
"What flowers grow up there?" I asked.
"The never finished kind," he laughed.
Soon he'd go under. But then, "new poems."

1.

Boots above all. Slack-skinned throats, cracked
deeply enough anything gets in, stays, the sluice
of years stains a good gumshoe reads like destiny,
those nubby rubber bottoms mostly kneaded smooth
where earth wanted a touch here, another there,
the way life goes. We live long enough we need
to pitch so many years, so much unspent tread.
But hold them, heft floats back, the slogging way
the heart felt, air thick as blood, that wood-like rut
where a puffing walk should have done, but didn't.

2.

The body's play, old friend, leaped on. Who stayed?
Tennis shoes, sneakers, the team: blue Pumas,
cat-carriers, quick and light as you, twenty-six.
Adidas, mud-muddled, the daily daubs of paint
on rooms long moved-from, your signature models.
Wilson basic as fifties' baths. Reebok, cushioned pillows
left humped shoulder to shoulder, fouled like sheets.
New Balance, stout Germans, swollen, unworkable.
Converse? Where? Dark middens eyes won't go in,
heel-starred, hoppers, slim-soled daddies. Where?

3.

Blacks, whites, scuffed, bad days suffered, worn,
slipped into same as Horace on his far-out farm,
friends who might have said with a tone, a style
you'd know at once, no question. How they accept
the weighty, walling-out thing you are and push
forward, whatever weather, tells their kind.
Some will fold, some soak up the chill and seep.
One or two might bite, provoked, or ill-used.
Yet each waits, dogged as a dog. Who knows what
good they keep? Some, in briared moonlight, may yet dance.

4.

Behind these no idea shapes the space, just dirt.
Dark that never fades, the funky smell of scraping
by, the feathery rip and blister of memory dried but
loosed, the angry knot, the broken boat without tie
or mooring, loafers in the cosmos of lost pilgrims.
Easy to see nakedness here, feel nail-thrust. Choose
elsewhere, they shrug, mute, the unchaste tongues
all that wags when we remember where they went,
like poets, once handsome as gods. They don't answer
no matter what we've asked. They're empty, open-eyed.

COMING DOWN IN OHIO

i.m. William Matthews

My uniform hung Air Force blue, way uncool,
when first we met, but Italian silks fit you
sleek as a summer shower. Tall and thin,
Gauloises, Yale swagger, you were the rule
exceptions were made to break. Years unkind

to say the least wiped out that grin I still see
when you lounged like Rimbaud, maudit.
Blond coeds drooled and took notes.
You quoted Horace, charmed us, sipped chablis
like gospel, cooed over Monk, bloomed in smoke

killing Hugo and Wright, lungs gone black.
Thirty-some, you sagged by noon, the slack
red set of your eyes, stride gimpy, stiff—
exactly what you'd lived to enact,
a boy-poet, rich as Dickens, keelhauled by life.

The more you aged, the more booze, pills, crunch
of poets got you. No jazz played too much
or kept the night-glooms off. You loved one
woman for looks, one art, one touch
as cool as grace you envied and easily took on.

You praised long fingers, NBA centers, pianists.
Both ranked only just lower than trumpets.
You played some yourself, slow forward
I recall, and argued game as well as any theorist.
Watch his elbows, Plumly groaned. I'd been warned,

and still you swiped my ball and nicked my face
enough to let me know the penalty of place
applies anywhere we play with lines
exactly. The last time I saw you you laced
up shoes, chair-bound, breathless, sweating in sun.

Then you died. I took it hard. Gone the you
friends and I had read, and would half be, half-tunes
half-heard, the slick easy heartbeat
whose dribble and leap was smoothly you.
But memory knows who you were on the concrete.

Maybe that's why I can't read unguarded elegies
where, almost, you walk on water. Silly.
I'm in a photo with you rising for a layup.
Your hand seems at the rim; beneath your feet
there's only air, the slab, nothing to disrupt

what looks, given this angle, perfect and casual.
Just the way you liked things. Dusk, marginal
as a zone, holds the rest of us stunned.
See, our mouths are open as if we sing choral
tributes as you rise, sexy star, razor-quick, alone.

Understanding how hurt scores, you always clowned,
as here you grin, float, beating our shouts
Time's up! The photo's pale,
but your look's locked past the ball as down
your body comes among us, who cry foul, most foul.

Two sets down, sweat-soaked, air too thin this high,
we sit on hot asphalt rehearsing shots almost made.
I lean back to watch one red-tailed hawk and another
in close swoops, at play in their blue idea, gliding,

wired-in to all, all above the earth only what they need.
Everything tumbles, unlinked more than we can think
or answer with our age-tuned moves but still I envy
practiced covert-tilts, scapulas tremoring in wind's touch,

body so effortlessly right, feathery buffet it slides on,
the plume through and leap past hard air that lifts jets
even water can't hold up, that *this* and *this* and *this*
they do for nothing except what nerve and eye-glint

want, a dive and float that make the joy of life. Now
what game's played? Remember Arizona—we were
young, feathery moves, a tournament of poets, Steve,
Galway, Coleman, Marvin, Bill, dead, playing, reading?

Serious weight seems all over me as I think of them.
I replay my old dreams, a boy's arms out, flying,
saying no word, alone, knowledge the feeling of it.
Then your racquet's whack, my arrowing ball is right,

the eye goes, catches, it back-soars, heart steady on,
and that way you look, when I surprise you, a little
older, slowed, your feet spread, but open to receive.
Harder! as Beowulf spoke to his sword, and it answered.

They hawk the yard, heaving big beaks,
laborers with picks, hoes, mattocks,
black all over them the formal suits
something has taught them to hang up
in bright air, brushed to sleekest shine,
and worn with the insouciance of rakes.

They do not grunt or moan or sigh, they
groom the grass like barbers, artful care
wielded with the moves of the gifted.
A few bump their bellies and flutter,
noisy squawks just inches off the dirt,
a kind of laugh they share about shade

other, prettier birds seem assigned to.
But they will not trade, or give no sign
any change digs at them. They tread
in power and numbers a particular line
of work everything else respects. Eyes
each offer, baleful, black, turned on you,

usually the gaze of chance. If swirled
aside, missing you, like driving drunks,
meteor fragments from cosmo-space,
you are no one, they've let you think.
Until your limbs bend, and you notice
they've scoured your yard. Then, wheeled

necks rotating, big mechanical claws,
hell's noise unsheathed, they will
bring quiet that's like a blanket.
Soon sparrows, wrens gulp, go still.
Cardinals stand dingy best alert.
Hard sun boils up blessed, black yawns.

I admire the whip of their wings in the sun, whorish pink
of feathers, above all the strut nonchalant in capes
tackier than Key West sunset, as if, baby, what else
waits for us but walking on water and pink landscapes?
A life we chose once, never then thinking of kids,
pensions, the awful news the papers pimp for sales.
Our TV's weekend nature show brings it back in flicks

of flamingoes swirled like semen, frantic for a quiet cove,
a mind confused as seed passion-blown. After it swirls,
it blithely drops lurid feathered bodies everywhere, no
hole or hump resistible, long Rockette legs uncoiled,
high breasts. A few bright boys troll for the weakest.
Some mate, some dissidents argue and spit. A callow
knob-kneed youngster trips alone, dipper-neck that probes

brown lake scum as if it gripped gold. This gruel, like God,
is mute and heavy, and her crowd's moving on. What
sign should we, voyeurs in the dark, give her? That black
snouts of crocks are coming? I watch her suck a carp
and half-twirl, slim as Bolshoi's best, moves sublime,
a sequined dancer aloof on neon streets we've walked,
hot pink wings lifting her from the ordinary suck of mud.

RODEO POKER

Angola, Louisiana

They train in the dark, pulling long muscles of their calves
for speed, for quickness to live, pushing up bodies on stone

that knows what prison they're in, some crying little secrets,
breath they can't hold, some mute as concrete, sweat pooling

until all shines in the corridor's light, thinking then the horn
rises, ivory as a child's tooth, trying to feel what they have

heard, slurp of flesh as it goes in, lightness, the flying corpse.
All the time they train, grins stride slowly across the faces

of guards, trustees, visitors who will wait tiered in the burn
of that afternoon that comes on. Some smell the tiny pores

closing, opening like a woman's sex. The broken ones say,
hardening, they strain to forget that nightmare. They roll fists

with steel weights as if, curls bobbing up to shaved chests,
they summon the gods of memory. They stand, breathe, sit.

This is how it is, asshole-tight at the table, alone in sand:
four players, cards held close, no side-bet, young bull loosed,

inexplicable, one who can holding cash as the others run,
watching everything happen, again. Those from home risen

like ghosts will be eating, joking in stands. Then four, saints
almost, bees diving in cheek-sweat and eye-pool, sit solid.

Changing, they negotiate the smell and feel of becoming
light, an animal's breath lifting them, even fingers fluttering.

Son driving, wife asleep, we fly the interstate, southern woods
impenetrable mile by mile, past hunters' houses tucked far back.

Squads of cars speed like dreams we're in. Ahead, some flyers
cross, but I think too big, not birds, other shapes, funny, white

darts hurled by something invisible, loosed by desire, each
body focused, one ahead appearing to hold them together, lifted

on earth by lightness, speed our limbs do not know. Then two
burst like melons, a car wobbles, and stunned, as if shot, a face

sails on, as we do, driving in line, linked. A third dog stops,
decides for no reason we can see to come to us, and the head

like a summer tomato explodes. Two dawdlers, reaching green
center, skid, turn back, and behind float like butter in the sun's

boiling soup. Shaken, you bolt up from shallow sleep, full alive.
Like depression choosing which child to give up, this can't be

stopped until five comic charmers lie slicked on tarmac, bone
and vapor, and wake to ask what in God's name led them to us.

Slowed by what's happened, day holds its breath, dozes now;
we glide like nails ahead. What did they want? Don't dreams

have rules? You cry. You blink, mouth open. A band boils out,
vanishing as we float, family like any, some gone missing,

one place becoming another, dusk pale as hope. What do we do?
you cry to woods. I stare ahead, turn, glance inside, belted

self down, turn back to trees that limb by limb still hold
blackness we look into, driven, running along with the others.

Traffic clots, white-haired tourists gag the French Quarter.
In cars we sit, bizarre cold for New Orleans, full-blast
heater one minute, off the next, like love, hate,
menopause, bills, kids in therapy, booze, you can see it
flood the faces passing, stale breath of despair. That's why

I almost don't see Degas's tall stairs, his broody place
where old streets roll like water under live oaks, black limbs
twining like women's arms Matisse would dance to.
Painting's not escape she says, sitting at fogged glass
I wipe away to watch where Degas sat. Too much sun

drove him home to Paris, carting dreams, amour des noirs,
his tales of scandal starring us in flashed strokes,
him hanging in that back closet vest and manly
cravat, hungry but happy enough on Rue Misery
where naked legs in season hang yet at open windows.

Walkers scrape their battered shoes and brick walks buckle.
Eighteenth-century clapboard puckers its pastel, knots
of magnolia leaves kicked aside hiss again, boats
we all imagine disembarking that one new goddess.
He'd grin when a good-looking one turned in his way.

I like this riding, thinking of good legs, underparts moist,
papery with little gold hairs, Degas leaning to propose
at stoop, painting from the heart with what you'd think
no feeling at all, just color filling in time. So: gloves
off, he greets her, cash passes, and numb hours like joy.

Same Louisiana sky today pressing like body weight.
Degas won't give up, nudging left, right, her ease
a pulse in his hands. Bodies float where he lives,
their faces toward the river's mucky flow, boats
low by cafés he'll be sketching her likeness in for beer.

THE QUAIL MEN OF CHURCHLAND

For Jeddie Smith

They loved Cary farm, Everwine's that hadn't been owned
by Everwine in memory. Harvested rows flew up coveys

like dust as Big Bruce's blue truck, wobbling, banged forth
the one joy-filled body we spilled from, lying as men do

to find things alive among us. There was somebody's joint
they stopped in, back-whacking jokes, whistled hellos, bets

hustled, smoke. Then chair-scrape, fingertip on a boy's arm.
They'd whip out the two-lane, all piled up with red beans,

bread, potato soup not soup, maybe not even potato. Odor
of coffee, bragging on bird dogs they cast, mailbox names

read as they went walking like gents, telling all they could
not ever explain. I'd bounce in front, crying tell me again

how birds arrowed up air, falling like gifts, black Peanut's
trailer Bruce owned in field's middle, and Peanut drunk, pen

knife waving like a sword, begging, wife gone, work gone,
booze gone, boy Robert gone, Vietnam, that never came back.

Behind my tall son, shade-drowned, dog-wag close, gun
broke, I remember I was the boy they fell behind, path gone

blank as knowing, chill night where I walked on fern, stars,
leading them home, their breath blooming loud last dreams.

How silent, then, star-fields. I wanted those growls of love,
words hearts beat for, touch of fathers, a tall son. *Save us!*

George's boy screamed, in the Sea of Japan again. Quiet
hurts, Uncle George said, firing if a cornstalk shook, houses

looming like sharks. I'd call, bird's down! In woods or swamp,
I'd say; if dogs false-pointed, I'd say. Big Bruce cried out,

Birds won't go in holes! Dogs did. George soothed, *Careful,
Careful!* Then wham, wham. *My bird!* Bruce grabbing it up,

laughs wheezing, me dreaming I'd done it, feathers in sun.
Day would come at last to not much, words worn weightless

as souls, thin, waiting for what happens. They'd stand before
Peanut's trailer, light flicker inside. Soon silver bourbon cups,

clink-clink, all divvied, Bruce holding Peanut's hand, a joke
freckling them with tears. Wanting what? How little I knew.

Now, game bag heavy, I hear my feet pad, my son leading,
stars like teeth at pines. My throat burns with dust, so I ask,

why did we blow the birds away and drink midnight's air?
Old Lovies, what cry keeps the field alive? Tell me again.

LITTLE BOATS, UNSALVAGED

For Fran & Ellen Voigt

Thwarts, chines, ribs mud-caked, this one's deadrise bow is lifted
as if by gusts, whitecaps' scud and swat no fear in her. Would she

plane, or plow? Give a good ass-bumping if we'd go out today?
Someone left his dream-sized hull to salt's pitting slosh, a girl's

name time rubbed from a tide-canted stern. Mahogany's rotted,
worm-grained, beauty we schemed in side-yard sun. Where I live

marshes fill with them, dull wanderers stoned by trash, the fog-eye
of acid-mist. Mud flats, pocked, keep all half-sunk, half surged-up,

skiers flung off where a wheel whipped. Sun's char at pine-tops,
dying gullsong's where I go, and night's swell-in of black water.

In earshot, almost, when breasts boiled and peeled, scarred scalds
slipped under. Nail-bleed, sun-bleach say no set-out days left. Still,

I find it here, floating and leap-in, sway of grass like joy as we
buoyed up, or plunged into holes, refusing to be anchored and safe,

little go-hard twist of an outboard screwing for all we'd make up,
guess at, going God knows where—some sandbed like a room, calm

so lucid nothing could be lost, keys quick as fish-darts, no rings
that joined what we'd cast into. But wading might be a sliced sole,

oyster's edge, panic's throttled shudder, wind squealing hurt.
Breath sucked again, I look past all that storms destroy at hands

in mine, steps by hooks rusting, moments of love with cooler
beer-stuffed, shells opening, flesh brine-perfect, still pumping.

Somewhere charts know, we're shoving out, so happy we weep.
How quietly, then, it happened, salt coating us, sun like fingers

raking the cheeks, the unsalvaged hull alive with swirls of stars.
Like a child I still climb in and wait to be lifted, flood tide cycling

in tiny waves that swell, take us unaware, the sprawl and soothe
of reed bed, wake bubbling, anticipation, all we loved. *This. Now.*

IV

PLOWMAN

For Terry Hummer

. . . the little trawler Anna May, which went to pieces on Diamond
Shoals at the height of a severe storm December 9, 1931.
—DAVID STICK, *The Graveyard of the Atlantic*

Me bifel a ferly . . .
—WILLIAM LANGLAND, *Piers Plowman*

What I know of death you never told me, a man
who fell out of his life, his farmyard, magnolia shade
where a '49 Ford coupe goes on rusting, and dogs
that die or do not seem doomed to bark at the moon.
And of God, who owns all the hardware, and time
that rusts or breaks it, you have kept full silence.

All I have of you is the tale of why you plowed
perfect lines in a plot not a football field long, no
crop ever grown, no sauce for that dirt, just turn
and counter-turn, a vision working, and I saw you
hardly at all, who entered me, little shadow of a man,
but enough today I watch crows swirl and plume

from the sky that sees all, and I ask what you knew
nights when, maybe, you whooped too much to live
with townsmen, days you followed what lines said,
mule towing your point up and down, your blade
brightly peeling what might have been one chance
to swim into the light with the other lives redeemed.

God knows where it starts, feet on the cold wet dark
of the morning, wind spit, all the before-years nothing,
for mullet now race wavetips, your own lips shiver
that a woman once begged to lie against for the heat
of the sun in them, and blue, out there, swells, ticks,
it heaves and bangs your boat's bottom. It will leave

you alone, but not forever. At twenty, some already
stood stumps, scorned by net draggers, docked,
once boys, and you tithed them a wage you carried
in a can, yours dumped on home shelf, the woman
chopping and stewing the day-end sweetness, giving
your flesh luck's haw and heave a man sets out for. But,

not forever. From Hampton to the Shoals, dark engines
made your lank legs shake, spine shudder like sea-trout,
silver skimmers just under the sea-skin, and dream
to see, in that far-off gazing way a man looks on lines
of the shore fading, the future, its drawing about you
then what hands might hold, breath steady and paced,

the nets played, slow-dragged where the scabbed dead
angrily slipped your bag, stinking sea-swales, so many
the Graveyard seemed like a city of hulls at harbor, you
surfing over, prop wash like new dawn clearing, then
freed, wheels raced, scooped fish-cash treasure gold
in sun and silver's furious liquid. So home again. Until

a day rain rasped and rang in a bad wind's raking. Here
blew bottom up bare, and beat boats down on it hard,
men and good wood gouged, stove-edged, nail-pops
like darts, keel in like a sexed dog storm-screwed, air
rotting inside whooshed out, weight like years unused.
You were a mouth of sand grinding in snow-fall of fish.

But not forever, if you could winch up the whipping
mast, make it to the top-crossed stretchers, be nailed
arm and leg there, razored by line-flay, water-divoted,
borne in wind-highs to see what way a man can live
when change claws and fate will show no solid step.
So that was what you did, ice-blistered. But saw *what*

up clung inside the needle and hack-back of blackness,
sand-spidered, swollen in wet plummet's spike and go?
Like womb-wrench no God mapped, no compass sourced.
Here's how I think of the next: green stalk-hair, pale

gold-fall on grasses, new, at slate sand, like a woman's
sway, and surf-plod, day's glassed mists like faces where

waves plead leaving sand-lines like mules making
strides, that phosphorescent gash awash, the weather
coming, going while you, above, swayed, did cry out
as if worlds went. But when ghost-faces came, left,
toed surf-snarl, shrugged, backs beetled homeward,
what words then? Who, hung alive, forgives who here?

You did, Plowman, walk that water of belly-up death.
Skin like dried varnish peeled on the mast-pole; you
lifted away meat-raw hands. But not forever. Came
down, lay in boat, neat corpse-carrier, heard words
wisp and settle over you like the charms of the priest,
whom you sneered off, as seas rustled. What a future

to live remembering what been doled to you, deft
and durable a man you had to be, and are inside me
still when I think how you lugged your armful of sky
coolly down, blinking it inside behind swelled eyes,
salt-crusted as creatures skittering to live, the awful
falling tons of night dark sprawled, hard, moon-cleaned,

ground there to stride upon and smell, and later in bed
to rise from the woman, afraid, and go dressed in suit.
Then I came, stood in my school's window, set noses
of students to read, and found you: black clad in sun,
shirt tipfoam white, tie black as wet rope, hidden
under big brimmed shade-hat, Homer of parallel lines

you cast forth with mule's help, a stepping determined
like star-tracks, up to the road, back, pace dependable
as wall-tick or peach blossom or heart's shrug. Lunch
at log's fall, bread, croaker, I guessed, her hand-gift
plain as wax-papered wrap and bag in coat pocket.
No drink. Then next puffs of dust, mule-risen, man

walking the dirt, off water forever, off townsmen too,

who'd not hang hats by yours, or go paths down swamps
where boys at gunnels smoked, leaned, lied, learned
how the black weep of things never ends, just courage.
I'd hear your tale over fists of whiskey, dull cousins
fishing for whys, that sorrow flushed you like wave-grit,

or guilt that flips and scuttles a man when friends go.
Maybe shame. Not fear. For gutless these were not, nor
mockers of seas, who shook at wave-work as you,
Plowman, did. Yet you failed, we knew it. But not
forever, for who can climb past hard-holding earth?
I left; you died. Few remember Plowman's place, but

dream's small seed clings where winters pile upon me.
I see at last green slopes like a girl waving, gold-hair
of the flying sun. White snow-arms in furrows feel
first shouldering-up of stalks, daffodils like legs
unfold, sway, face light that redeems whatever is cut
under wind, sand, or night's star-glide and heel-strike.

You turned to the courage of living, a hunger to rise past
eyes that will not open, ears jammed by sound-shrill
of the dead's "Here endeth. . . ." Like you walking lines,
outgoings and incomings the same, I look through
windows for the less and less that lives. I do not yet
know what you knew but no hour bests dawn-glow

on lips, woman or mule, as they breathe in open fields.
As you did with love's face in your hands, help me
tell again that story, what lines, hand-hold and rung,
gave the saving step, as you had it, and made it,
down that pole to green's glistening. Walk on. Sun's
coming, mule I am saying, go ahead now, turn, return.